Getting the Most Out of Your Homeschool This Summer

Learning Just for the Fun of It!

Lee Binz,
The HomeScholar

First Printing, 2015

Printed in the United States of America

ISBN: 1512356719
ISBN-13: 978-1512356717

Getting the Most Out of Your Homeschool This Summer

Learning Just for the Fun of It!

What are Coffee Break Books?

Getting the Most Out of Your Homeschool This Summer is part of The HomeScholar's Coffee Break Book series.

Designed especially for parents who don't want to spend hours and hours reading a 400-page book on homeschooling high school, each book combines Lee's practical and friendly approach with detailed, but easy-to-digest information, perfect to read over a cup of coffee at your favorite coffee shop!

Never overwhelming, always accessible and manageable, each book in the series will give parents the tools they need to tackle the tasks of homeschooling high school, one warm sip at a time.

Everything about these Coffee Break Books is designed to suggest simplicity, ease, and comfort - from the size (fits in a purse), to the font and paragraph length (easy on the eyes), to the price (the same as a Starbucks Venti Triple Caramel Macchiato). Unlike a fancy coffee drink, however, these books are guilt-free pleasures you will want to enjoy again and again!

Table of Contents

Introduction

The Living is Easy!

Summer is my favorite season! It's a time when priorities turn to camping, vacation, snuggling young children, relaxing in a hammock, and reading great books. Have some watermelon, throw something on the grill, and enjoy the water. It's important to take a break and spend some time relaxing so you are refreshed. Summertime ... the living should be easier!

Some homeschoolers school the whole year round, while some follow the school calendar. But ALL homeschoolers need to take a break, whether it's vacation weeks during the school year or the summer off. You should NOT feel guilty taking a break, and in fact it will make your homeschool better.

Summer can provide an opportunity to work on all those tasks you put off throughout the school year. It's easier in the summer to catch-up on little things, such as cleaning out the closet under the stairs, teaching your four-year-old to tie her shoes, or planning a visit to grandparents in another state.

Summer's warm, lazy days are also a great opportunity to catch up on homeschool tasks you have put off during the school year. When you're consumed with helping your children focus on their studies, little things such as record keeping, reading lists, and planning courses for next year can seem completely overwhelming. Summer is the best time to tackle your lists and get ready to face the fall with confidence and anticipation.

For Christian homeschoolers, there's a Biblical mandate for rest. You should not be working 24/7 on school or doing schoolwork the whole year round without a break. The Bible is clear that there is a time for rest. There are also physiological reasons for rest. Sleep is important because it helps your children grow. Rest allows your brain to process your activities each day and rejuvenate your body.

Even if you're taking an official break, learning still happens. Children are curious. They are natural learners. They will learn even if they don't intend to. Your goal during the summer isn't to prevent children from learning. Your goal is to take a break from your regular work. Encourage independent learning and use summer for a time of relaxed learning!

The ideas in this book will help you make the most of your summer and help prepare you to resume the race with energy in the years to come!

Chapter 1

When to Take a Break

Summertime means different things to different homeschool families — some keep working right through the summer because they take breaks throughout the year, and others take the whole summer off because they've had their noses to the grindstone all year. When should you stop? How do you know? As with many homeschool decisions, it all depends on your family.

You'll know your family needs a break if you notice the "natives are getting restless." If your children are starting to act up, they're just not cooperating the way they used to, and you're seeing a little bit more attitude, then those are signs it's time for a break.

Course Completion

The completion of courses also signifies it's time for a break. However, if you're concerned that your child has not fully completed their science book, keep in mind how they handle this in both private and public schools. As long as students have finished 75-80% of the textbook, they have completed the course for the year; they don't have to consider it a failure at all. In the same way, if you have completed 75% of what you set out to do, it's okay for you to consider it done for the year.

When public and private school teachers begin the year, they often have the freedom to say, "I'm going to skip these two chapters" in a textbook so they can complete the course in one school year. Likewise, if your natives are getting restless, and you have completed 75% of your curriculum, you can legitimately consider that course complete.

Another way to measure completion is using the number of hours required for a credit. If you have worked for one hour or more per day or if you have 120-180 hours of work done in the subject, you can record that your child has earned the credit, and is DONE for the year. Often, the curriculum is so full of books, worksheets and information that your children don't finish in a year. This can also happen when parents supplement or add to the curriculum. If you are ready to be done for the year and you have put in the time, you don't need to continue working until you have finished every assignment or book, you can just call it complete.

Core Subjects

Some core subjects are easy to finish and others, such as math and science, take daily effort. When you fall behind in these subjects, it's difficult to catch up. You can let non-core subjects drop when you are done for the year. In high school, instead of granting a whole credit, you can give your child a half credit for foreign language and just stop for the year. Math is unique, though; I encourage you to work through the summer if necessary to finish at least 80% of the math book. It will be more difficult to understand math the following year without finishing the book. Colleges want to see four credits of math. It's important to teach a whole class each year.

Mastery

You can also base completion of courses on mastery of the concepts. Sometimes students already know some of the academic content, without having read the textbook. If you give a test that demonstrates your student has mastery over a concept, such as a final exam or an SAT or AP exam, you can go ahead and consider that course finished.

Burnout

The enthusiasm and energy level of your student can be a strong indicator of whether or not you're done. If your child is still gung-ho and you can squeeze a little more study time out of them, then perhaps you can keep going for a few more weeks. If, however, your student is burnt out, you will just be beating your head against the wall if you continue to press them for more.

The same is true of teacher burnout. If you as a teacher can just barely tolerate homeschooling, it's time to prioritize your mental health. If you have finished 75% of the work and need a mental health break, it's okay to call an end to study time.

Anger can sometimes become an issue, for both the child and the parent. It's important to be honest with one another and acknowledge when there's a problem. Pushing through when relationships are not going well typically leads to ineffective learning. If you find that student or teacher burnout or anger is making your homeschooling less and less effective, it's best to take a break.

Natural Consequences

Sometimes kids just don't do the work needed during the school year. They don't work enough, don't put in the hours, and NEED to get that core class done. When that happens, summer school is a natural consequence of not getting their work done. Assign core subjects during the summer until the work is done. As the kids are working, make a plan to prevent the problem from happening again next year. Remember my two big tips for schoolwork consistency next year. First, have a meeting with your child every day to check in on each subject and make sure they stay on task. Second, put weak areas first, so the subjects they are most likely to "forget" are done first each day.

Taking a break in the summer is important. Even if your child must take summer school classes at home, that doesn't mean Mom or Dad needs to work, too. Have them work independently so you can get a break from the normal rigors of homeschooling. Breaks are a breath of fresh air that can rejuvenate your homeschool next fall!

Alternatives

Taking a break is not an all-or-nothing situation. You don't have to choose between schoolwork for eight hours every single day or stopping school and never touching a book or piece of paper for the summer. You can find a middle ground. You can stop working on English or spelling, but choose to keep working on math, especially when you are dealing with burnout. Burnout stings like a sunburn. It aches like a pulled muscle. It stinks like a teenager after a weeklong mission trip. Stopping schoolwork, or just some particular subjects, for a while may be just the break you need to regroup and get ready to start anew later.

You're the parent and you know your children and your situation. Make the choices that will serve your family the best.

Lee Binz, The HomeScholar

Chapter 2

Summer Record Keeping Catch Up

One of the most important tasks for homeschool parents to keep up with is high school records. Even if you're a gifted home educator or you have great intentions, you must follow-through! You have to do the work of keeping records.

Keep records of activities that are academic in nature or at the high school level. Because it's relatively common for homeschoolers to work on high school level classes at a young age, if your junior high child is doing algebra right now, keep tabs on it. Algebra is a high school level course, which means you can put an algebra course on the high school transcript even if it is completed before high school.

Homeschool Transcripts

Once your student reaches high school, record keeping should include creating course descriptions and transcripts that capture all their educational experiences in terms colleges can understand. A course description is a simple paragraph describing what you taught. You can create course descriptions using a textbook, catalog, or homeschool book description, or simply by writing a list of what your student did in the course. This might seem daunting unless you start small. Try to write one course description each day while your child is busy with summer activities, or write one a week if they're at home and underfoot. After the first few tries, you'll find yourself turning them out in no time!

For more help on creating professional looking course descriptions for your student, check out my Comprehensive Record Solution at:

www.ComprehensiveRecordSolution.com

Reading Lists

You are not the only one who can work on homeschool records during the summer; get your kids involved, too! While you work on course descriptions, your children can help with the next summer homeschool task — reading lists! This is just a list of books your children have read, including title and author. Often requested by colleges, and sometimes useful for scholarship applications, reading lists are an important part of your student's high school record. Include books you have assigned your children to read over the summer, books they've used in their coursework, and books they read just for fun.

Encourage your children to keep track of their own reading, if possible.

Unfortunately, no matter what I did or said, my children didn't seem able to keep their own lists. They were excellent readers and were thrilled with reading, but they had absolutely no interest in creating a reading list for me. I had my children bring me stacks of the books they read and added to their list each week. Do what works for your family; the important thing is to make a list.

Planning

Another important summer activity is to plan ahead for the next school year. Summer is when you should be purchasing curriculum and developing your schedule and goals for the coming school year. If you have a middle or high school student, think about what courses they'll need to cover in order to get into college. If you schedule the upcoming school year now, you can encourage independent learning in the fall — just give them the schedule to follow!

Continuing Education

The last thing to keep in mind this summer is that you are a professional educator. Consider your own need for continuing education, too. Perhaps you can attend a homeschool convention or buy books and videos that will help you be a better home educator. Invest in yourself. This is your chosen profession and it's worth the effort. Remember to include a little rest and relaxation. Don't worry if you're a little behind on homeschool tasks. Summer is here and it's the best time to catch up. Think about how great you'll feel when the fall comes around and you're ready to roll!

Chapter 3

Delight Directed Summertime Learning

Summertime is a great time to incorporate a little of what I call delight directed learning. Delight directed learning is kids pursuing interests that come naturally to them. If your child has been longing to go to a health care camp or dive into a new orchestra performance, that's delight directed learning. For many kids, this learning comes in the form of sports. Other kids will do nothing but read books. Some kids will do volunteer work, perhaps serving as a candy striper at a hospital. Some kids love working with children and need to earn money, so they travel to different Vacation Bible Schools, helping at various churches. Other kids will work on the majority of their club projects, for Scouts or 4-H.

Give Gifts

One way you can encourage delight directed learning is by using summer as a gift-giving opportunity. You can give your children gifts that will encourage their interests. For one of my sons, I bought *The Great Courses* classes on economics and American government. If you give gifts that encourage your children's interests, it could help spark a passion that leads to great things.

Mentors

Encourage your child's summertime delight directed interests by finding mentors for them, perhaps through clubs and colleges. People often have better availability during the summer, and may be more willing to spend time mentoring young people.

Depending on your child's special interest, try doing a search online for a specific term, such as "ornithology clubs." You can also contact small, friendly colleges to find a helpful professor. Ask around at church and other community groups to see if you can find an adult with the same interests. It took a LONG time before we found a mentor in economics for my son. The first two we tried weren't a good fit, but they eventually led to a great professor who took my son under his wing. Ask yourself, if you shared that interest as an adult, how would YOU find a way to meet like-minded people?

Margin

Delight directed learning requires time. If your child's life is too full and has no margin, they won't be able to pursue their interests. The book *Margin* talks about how important it is to have space in your life:

> "Margin is the space between our load and our limits and is related to our reserves and resilience. It is a buffer, a leeway, a gap; the place we go to heal, to relate, to reflect, to

recharge our batteries, to focus on the things that matter most."

Books have a lot of white space. The more white space on the page, the easier it is to read the book. This premise is true for life as well. The more unplanned white space on the page of your life, the more room there will be for what matters.

If your child never has the time and space to try new things (or you never encourage them), they might miss the discovery of a new interest. Summer is a great time to start exploring your child's delight, because there's more free time. Don't forget to carry the concept of margin into your regular school year, too.

Colleges and Scholarships

Colleges love to see students who have unique interests or skills. They get tired of the same old cookie cutter students and welcome unique applicants. Use your child's unique gifts to help them stand out from the crowd, and perhaps even sow the seeds for a lifetime pursuit or career. In addition, your child's unique interests and gifts can lead to college scholarships. There are scholarships out there for piano players, filmmakers, debaters, you name it! If your child finds a passion during the summer and follows up on it during the school year, it will translate into great courses on the transcript and will help scholarship applications rise to the top.

Just Fun?

During both the summer and the school year, it's a good idea to include as much delight directed learning as possible. It isn't because we want school to be easy or fun, but because we want it to be interesting and applicable. When school is interesting, students will learn more, and they will begin to LOVE learning. We included self-directed courses in our homeschool. Critical thinking, public speaking, occupational education, and Russian history were all included in one of my son's records. My other son took self-directed courses in economics, microeconomics, macroeconomics, business law, psychology, and marketing.

Here are some ideas for classes and activities you could include as part of self-directed summer learning:

- short, daily review with independent study
- field trips
- assigned newspaper readings
- have your child keep a journal
- fill an educational gap, such as brushing up on typing skills
- short unit study to fill small gaps
- math review
- foreign language review
- reading
- games for the love of learning

It's important to organize your summer. Small doses of summer school prevent your home from descending into chaos. Tidbits of reading, writing, and math will help children retain what they learned during the homeschool year. Experts agree that foreign language study requires daily use of the language.

Don't think "school" though. Consider this a short time of day when children are occupied independently while you are working on household chores. Create a simple checklist for each day.

Take advantage of delight directed learning by enrolling your children in summer camps and activities they can enjoy and learn through, such as:

- music classes
- art classes or camps
- volunteering (clothing bank, food bank, Vacation Bible School at church)
- Boy Scouts or Girl Guides
- 4-H
- clubs
- sports

Camp on a Transcript!

Don't forget to capture summer camp activities on your child's high school transcript! Add up all the hours. If your child is at camp for two weeks, eight hours a day, for ten days, that adds up to

80 hours, which is a half credit. For example, if it were a computer science camp then you could consider it a half credit in "Computer Science."

Remember, not everything needs to be separated on the transcript. You can distribute credit hours among a number of courses on the transcript. An acting camp may not be restricted to the theatre arts. Some of it may be considered part of an English credit, such as part of your child's Shakespeare studies. Summer camps can also be included on the activity list.

Learning Just for the Fun of It!

It's possible for kids to learn JUST because they love it! Your job as parent is to pick up the mess they leave behind, and turn it into a wonderful course description showing what they have learned. I think that's the best kind of learning! Remember the TV show, "Mr. Roger's Neighborhood"? Fred Rogers once said:

"Play is often talked about as if it were a relief from serious learning. But for children, play is serious learning. Play is really the work of childhood."

At the high school level, play is delight directed learning and a source of high school electives.

Chapter 4

Summer School Options

Summer is a great time to learn about new and different topics (outside of your usual homeschool curriculum), in small, easy-to-digest bites. One summer when my boys were younger, we spent just 30 minutes a day on a unit study about health. Other years, we worked on projects such as mapping the states and capitals, or learning how to type. We even spent one summer working on educational computer games! My kids laughed whenever I assigned them a game, but there are great, educational, math and science computer games out there!

Foreign Language Fun

Believe it or not, studying a foreign language is also a great summertime activity. Learning a foreign language is a lot of work, so we practiced for fifteen minutes a day and enjoyed watching DVDs with subtitles. Some great children's movies out there are dubbed in foreign languages. For instance, if you're studying French, watch *Finding Nemo* in French and read the English subtitles or watch it in English and read the French subtitles. Sometimes children will memorize the whole narrative of their favorite movie because they've seen it so many times. It's easy for them to translate it in their heads if they watch it in a foreign language!

Review Math

Summer is a great time to work on math review. We worked on math for fifteen minutes a day over the summer, using my favorite book, *Math Flash*; it's a tiny book that has three math problems on each page. I found three problems to be just the right amount for my kids in high school. It was just enough so they wouldn't complain and could keep their skills up over the whole summer. If you can't find *Math Flash* in your local bookstore, look for a math review book. Even if it is something easy, you can pull out a few problems each day for them to complete.

When your kids get into the upper math levels, the best book for math review is an SAT prep book. Another great option is to visit Khan Academy (www.khanacademy.org). With over 3,000 videos on everything from arithmetic to physics, and finance to history, this is an outstanding, free way to learn anything about K-12 math. Just make sure to record what your student learns, and include it on their high school transcript if they do high school level work!

Fill Gaps

If your family takes a break from regular academics during the summer, then it could be a good time to fill any educational gaps, whether in traditional areas such as math or in extra-academic areas.

Typing is an example of an extra-academic area, as is cooking and auto mechanics. These subjects might be outside of the typical curriculum's scope, but they are important skills. Summer is the perfect time to tackle them in small pieces, when you're not overwhelmed with the regular academics of the school year.

Sample Summer School Schedule

If you're unsure how much to work on over the summer, check out what we used to work on in our summer school schedule:

- Unit Study: 15-30 minutes independent reading
- Math: 15 minutes daily (e.g. 3-5 practice problems or one workbook page)
- Foreign Language: 15 minutes listening, speaking, or reading (pop in a DVD!)

- Reading: 15-30 minutes independent reading
- Writing: 15 minutes journal writing
- Educational games: 30 minutes of learning games (board games or computer-based)

This summer school schedule will give your child a total of about one to two hours of work a day during the summer to retain their skills. It won't take up much time for you as a parent, and will ensure you all have relaxation time and time for "doing nothing." For bonus points, incorporate games so learning includes giggles! Check out the article, "Play Your Way to a Great Vocabulary" on The HomeScholar website for more ideas.

Remember that excessive technology use can prevent or obstruct learning. Kids are so used to being entertained by various devices that they may not know how to entertain themselves. It's important to limit technology use to a reasonable amount throughout the school year but especially over the summer. Find tips and ideas for setting boundaries by reading my article, "Setting Logical Boundaries on Technology with Your Teen" on The HomeScholar website.

Use Other Teachers

Most parents want to make summer fun and educational, but they don't want to create a lot of new work for themselves, after all, it's summer! That's where summer classes can help. Maybe you just haven't had time to squeeze in an art class and your child is interested in art, or perhaps you've always wanted them to experience team sports, but it just hasn't fit into your school year. Summer is the time!

Perhaps you want your child to take a class to fill a specific learning gap. I talked to a mom recently whose child was not doing well in SAT math. She decided summer was a great opportunity to take an SAT prep class because somebody else would do the teaching and she would get a bit of a break. No matter your needs or your student's interests, there's sure to be an interesting class out there for your child!

Summer is also a good time for your children to join or form a club, or to do volunteer work. My husband and I worked at a local clothing bank for a long time, but there are also food banks and Vacation Bible Schools out there looking for volunteers. As an extra bonus, volunteer work makes a great addition to your student's portfolio when they start applying to colleges.

Write it Down

Journaling is another great summertime activity that's both fun and educational. I know many people who are successful with journaling. While they might not include journal writing as a subject during the school year, their children are willing to journal every day during the summer. This can help students with writing skills, and can be fun if you're traveling — whether camping, visiting a different area of the country, or just staying home.

If you do any summer learning, remember to capture it and turn it into school credit on your child's transcript. Some common summer credits include physical education and occupational education (which simply means working at a job). As you count credits, remember that between 120-180 hours of work is one credit, and 75-90 hours of work is a half credit. Perhaps your student is in an orchestra or a choir during the summer. You can just estimate those hours and say, "It looks like they're going to spend ten hours a week in class for the eight weeks of summer, which is eighty hours, or a half credit experience."

Learning doesn't only count when it happens during the "school year." Whenever and wherever your children learn, if it's at the high school level, you can count it towards their high school coursework.

Chapter 5

Save Money! Homeschool College This Summer!

I looked at the brochure for the test I was considering for my son, and immediately felt better. It said, "Who takes CLEP? A homeschooled 15-year-old." I felt so much better when I walked into the test center, knowing that my son couldn't be THAT unusual, since his demographic was right on the brochure. Imagine our surprise!

In no time at all, my son obtained college credit in "Principles of Marketing" and "Business Law" courses and I had never purchased curriculum! How does that happen, exactly? As homeschool parents, we usually know what our children have been taught, but we may not realize what they've learned! There is a place where knowledge reigns supreme, a place where you can also discover their hidden learning - your local CLEP testing center.

Why I chose CLEP exams

CLEP stands for College Level Examination Program, but in our home, we called it, "Can Lower Education Payments!" A successful grade on each exam can be worth three to six college credits, and can save you a BUNCH of money. Exams are approximately $65-$90 each, depending on where you take them, but that's inexpensive compared to the cost of college. Each exam can be prepared for at home, like any other homeschool course. Take exams all year round, even in the summer, five days a week at conveniently located testing centers. Almost every test is taken on a computer, and questions are all multiple choice. Each question is straightforward, not nuanced, because the exam is intended for non-traditional learners and you either know the answer or you don't. Many adult learners returning to college after a long time use CLEP - even moms! Two thousand nine hundred or more colleges nationwide accept CLEP exams and award college credit for each passing exam. There are at least 33 different subject exams.

The summer before my sons' senior year, we decided to begin homeschooling college with CLEP exams. We worked on them during the summer so that we could include passing scores in their college applications. Since their senior year would be at community college, I wanted to know which courses they could pass by examination so they wouldn't be bored in unnecessary college classes.

We started with a $20 investment in The College Board's *CLEP Official Study Guide*. To begin, I told my boys to look over the titles and see which test names they liked. I encouraged them to take the sample tests they were interested in, but to stop if they got frustrated. I reminded them that they only had to get 50% correct to pass the CLEP exam. The reason for this was simple: ALL the questions were difficult! I wrote each of their practice scores on the table of contents.

After my sons gained experience on a few sample tests, we decided to begin taking tests "for real," starting with their best subjects. The pre-test they scored highest in was American Government, so I bought a review book for the CLEP exam in that subject. The book I liked best for review was REA's *The Best Test Preparation for the CLEP*. They went through two or three more sample tests using that book and reviewing incorrect questions. At that point, my boys felt they were ready to try their first CLEP test.

The first time we arrived at the testing center, we paid a small fee to register with the technical college for a student number. Then the staff person led us to the testing area, where we paid the CLEP fee for the test. Unfortunately, the lone computer used for CLEP exams wasn't working, and the technical expert was not available to fix it. We waited for a whole hour but no technician arrived, so we drove home disappointed, without taking a test. When we arrived home, we received a phone call from the center explaining that the technician had plugged in the computer and it was finally working! How frustrating!

But we didn't give up! The next day we tried a different testing center at another technical college. When we arrived, we recognized a difference immediately. This testing center had over a dozen computers devoted to CLEP exams, so both of my kids could test at the same time. They also had technical help available on site. We had to pay a fee to register and get a student number again, and we had to pay a fee for the test. This time my kids were able to take the test. We were SO thrilled when they handed us the score reports that showed passing grades in a college course!

Our Homeschooling College Routine

After that first experience, we developed a family routine. Every Wednesday, we went to the testing center and took one or two tests. After they passed, with score reports in hand, we went out for lunch to celebrate. The next day, they decided on a new subject to tackle. In general, we went from their highest pre-test score and worked our way down. Every Thursday during the summer, we went to our local bookstore, and bought the REA study guide for the next subject. If you can't find these books, any AP or CLEP review book will work. My sons took a sample test each day and studied their incorrect answers. The following Wednesday, they took another CLEP exam. It was fun, and so satisfying to see college credits adding up!

One of my sons took and passed six CLEP exams, worth two quarters of college. The other son passed fifteen exams, earning the maximum one full year of college credit by exam. (Only nine exams were required to get one year of credit, but my son liked taking the tests!) Even for colleges that didn't give college credit for CLEP (and there are a few), the tests were still useful. One college they applied to required SAT II exams, which we didn't have. The CLEP exams were accepted instead. Even though the school didn't give college credit for CLEP tests, they still helped in the application process. The remaining tests helped my son place into upper division university classes.

Cumulative Learning or Intentional Learning

We planned homeschooling college as a way to document the cumulative learning of our homeschool. There is another way to homeschool college with CLEP exams, though. Your child can decide what subject they want to learn, and then intentionally study for the test. For example, my son Alex knew that psychology was required in college, but he just did NOT want to take it. My son was disgusted by Freud, and truly didn't want to hear his theories in a co-ed class. He tried taking the psychology

CLEP practice exam, but didn't pass. He begged me to buy him the REA study guide anyway. How could I refuse? He read the study guide from cover to cover, and then took the sample tests in the book until he felt comfortable. A few weeks later, he took and passed the Psychology CLEP exam, earned five college credits, and met the university requirement for psychology. He never had to take Psych in college, yet he still had the knowledge he needed to succeed.

Many colleges require outside documentation from homeschoolers. CLEP scores are delivered to colleges in the form of a transcript — the "love language" of colleges. It was just the way they liked it! You can choose to send scores to a college each time you take an exam, or you can wait and send all the scores at once, leaving out any scores you don't want. It was nice to have a transcript that supplemented my mommy-made transcript; it was a wonderful way to document my students' learning, whether they got college credit for it or not. When they got a passing score, I made sure to add "honors" to the high school course on their transcript. I figured if they knew a college amount of learning, they should at least be given high school honors credit for it.

For more information about CLEP exams, check The College Board website. If you are interested in more information about homeschooling college, check out *Accelerated Distance Learning* by homeschool graduate Brad Voeller. Consider homeschooling college this summer!

Chapter 6

College Preparation for Younger Homeschool Teens

Summer is a good time for parents of middle school students to begin thinking about high school preparation and college plans. You as a parent can make the future easier, and your younger student can plan for and think about high school, too. Even with young students, it's not too early to think about transcripts, course descriptions, and college visits. Plan ahead for the upcoming high school years this summer, and consider what you can do now to make things easier on you as a teacher.

Read Ahead

One of the ways you can prepare for the upcoming year is to read ahead. If your student will be reading a certain type of literature for school, then read it during the summer so you won't have to read during the school year, when things are busier. I did this when we were homeschooling, and it kept me sane. Start thinking about your student's future high school reading lists this summer, which are important to keep track of for college admissions. A librarian can help you find books from a variety of college bound reading lists. Check out the next chapter of this book as well.

Younger students can easily go on college visits during the summer. If your family is going on vacation, you could coordinate your vacation with any colleges you have in mind. For instance, if your child is interested in Hillsdale, and you're wondering what to do this summer, plan your vacation around a visit to Hillsdale so they can see what the campus is like. Most family finances don't allow for major vacations every year to track down different colleges, so if you can visit some colleges over the summer, it's a bit easier on the pocketbook. Although older students (sophomores, juniors, and seniors), will benefit from college visits during the school year, when they can take classes and get to know what college students are like, younger students may not want to sit in on a class because it could be way over their heads. In the summer, you can still visit colleges, see the campuses, and meet some professors. Your child may feel special because they're meeting professors and talking to them; it can make them feel grown up.

If you're thinking about homeschooling high school and applying for college, start planning now! There's great information and support available, and the sooner you start educating yourself, the easier the process will be.

Chapter 7

Summer Reading

Whether your family continues homeschooling through the summer or takes some time off, summer is a good time to include some purposeful reading. If you keep the mood light, the attitude fun, and choose great literature, you may be amazed at how much even reluctant readers begin to enjoy this fun summer pastime!

If books aren't a favorite, one way to encourage good reading habits is to have your child read the newspaper or a news magazine. This can help them get up to speed on what's happening in the world, since during the school year it's sometimes a little too busy to follow current events.

If you can encourage them to read books, below are two great reading lists, for middle school and college bound high school students.

Middle School Reading List

The following books are generally suitable for middle schoolers, ages 11-13. You can find the printable reading list here:

http://www.thehomescholar.com/pdf/ Middle-School-Reading-List.pdf

- Adams, Richard *Watership Down*
- Alcott, Louisa May *An Old-Fashioned Girl*
- Alcott, Louisa May *Little Women*
- Babbit, Natalie *Tuck Everlasting*
- Barrie, J.M. *Peter Pan*
- Bendick, Jeanne *Archimedes and the Door of Science*
- Blackwood, Gary *The Shakespeare Stealer*
- Bolt, Robert *A Man for All Seasons*

- Bunyan, John *The Pilgrim's Progress*
- Burnett, Frances Hodgson *The Secret Garden*
- Carroll, Lewis *Alice's Adventures in Wonderland*
- Carroll, Lewis *Through the Looking-Glass*
- Cather, Willa *My Antonia*
- Chesterton, G.K. *The Ballad of the White Horse*
- Cohen, Barbara *Seven Daughters and Seven Sons*
- Collier, James Lincoln *My Brother Sam Is Dead*
- Cushman, Karen *Catherine, Called Birdie*
- Daugherty, James *The Magna Charta*
- Defoe, Daniel *Robinson Crusoe*
- De Angeli, Marguerite *The Door in the Wall*
- Dickens, Charles *A Christmas Carol*
- Doyle, Arthur Conan *The Red-headed League*
- Ellis, Deborah *The Breadwinner* (3 book series)

- Farley, Walter *The Black Stallion* (series)
- Fitzgerald, John D. *The Great Brain*
- Fletcher, Susan *Shadow Spinner*
- Forbes, Esther Hoskins *Johnny Tremain*
- Frank, Anne *The Diary of a Young Girl*
- Freedman, Russell *Freedom Walkers: The Story of the Montgomery Bus Boycott*
- George, Jean Craighead *My Side of the Mountain*
- George, Jean Craighead *Tree Castle Island*
- Gipson, Fred *Old Yeller*
- Grahame, Kenneth *The Wind in the Willows*
- Henty, G.A. *In Freedom's Cause*
- Holling, Holling Clancy *Paddle-to-the-Sea*
- Hunt, Irene *Across Five Aprils*
- Jacques, Brian *Redwall Series*
- Juster, Norton *The Phantom Tollbooth*
- Keith, Harold *Rifles for Watie*

- Kipling, Rudyard *Captain Courageous*
- Kipling, Rudyard *The Jungle Book*
- Konigsburg, E.L. *From The Mixed-Up Files of Mrs. Basil E. Frankweiler*
- L'Engle, Madeleine *A Wrinkle in Time* (series)
- Lawrence, Caroline *The Roman Mysteries*
- Lee, Harper *To Kill a Mockingbird*
- Lewis, C.S. *The Chronicles of Narnia*
- Lindgren, Astrid *Pippi Longstocking*
- London, Jack *The Call of the Wild*
- London, Jack *White Fang*
- Lowry, Lois *The Giver*
- Lowry, Lois *Number the Stars*
- MacDonald, George *The Princess and the Goblin*
- MacLachlan, Patricia *Sarah Plain and Tall*
- McGraw, Eloise Jarvis *The Golden Goblet*
- Montgomery, L.M. *Anne of Green Gables* (series)
- Moody, Ralph *The Dry Divide*

- Naylor, Phyllis Reynolds *Saving Shiloh*
- Paterson, Katherine *Bridge to Terabithia*
- Paulsen, Gary *Hatchet*
- Peretti, Frank E. *The Cooper Kids Adventures* (series)
- Polland, Madeleine *Beorn the Proud*
- Pope, Elizabeth Marie *The Sherwood Ring*
- Pyle, Howard *Men of Iron*
- Pyle, Howard *The Story of King Arthur and His Knights*
- Pyle, Howard *Otto of the Silver Hand*
- Pyle, Howard and McKowen, Scott *The Merry Adventures of Robin Hood*
- Rawlings, Marjorie Kinnan *The Yearling*
- Rawls, Wilson *Where the Red Fern Grows*
- Robinson, Barbara *The Best Christmas Pageant Ever*
- Rogers, Jonathan *The Wilderking Trilogy*
- Sewell, Anna *Black Beauty*

- Speare, Elizabeth George *The Bronze Bow*
- Speare, Elizabeth George *The Witch of Blackbird Pond*
- Stevenson, Robert Louis *The Black Arrow*
- Stevenson, Robert Louis *Kidnapped*
- Stevenson, Robert Louis *Treasure Island*
- Sutcliff, Rosemary *The Eagle of the Ninth Chronicles*
- Tolkien, J.R.R. *The Hobbit*
- Twain, Mark *Adventures of Huckleberry Finn*
- Twain, Mark *The Adventures of Tom Sawyer*
- Verne, Jules *Twenty Thousand Leagues Under the Sea*
- Verne, Jules *Around the World in 80 Days*
- Wallace, Lew *Ben-Hur*
- Washington, Booker T. *Up From Slavery*
- White, T.H. *The Sword in the Stone*
- Wilder, Laura Ingalls *The Little House* (series)

- Williamson, Joanne *Hittite Warrior*
- Wyss, Johann David *The Swiss Family Robinson*

High School Reading List

The following books make great reading for college-bound high schoolers. You can find the printable reading list here:

http://www.thehomescholar.com/pdf/ College-Bound-Reading-List.pdf

American Literature

- Angelou, Maya *I Know Why the Caged Bird Sings*
- Cooper, James Fenimore *The Deerslayer*
- Cooper, James Fenimore *Last of the Mohicans*
- Crane, Stephen *The Red Badge of Courage*
- Douglass, Frederick *Narrative of the Life of Frederick Douglass*
- Fitzgerald, F. Scott *The Great Gatsby*

- Frank, Pat *Alas, Babylon*
- Franklin, Benjamin *The Autobiography of Benjamin Franklin*
- Haley, Alex *Roots*
- Hawthorne, Nathaniel *The Scarlet Letter*
- Hemingway, Ernest *A Farewell to Arms*
- Keller, Helen *The Story of My Life*
- Kennedy, John F. *Profiles in Courage*
- Lee, Harper *To Kill a Mockingbird*
- Lewis, Sinclair *Main Street*
- London, Jack *Call of the Wild*
- Malcom X, with Alex Haley *The Autobiography of Malcom X*
- Miller, Arthur *Death of a Salesman*
- Melville, Herman *Moby Dick*
- Paine, Thomas *Common Sense*
- Poe, Edgar Allan *Great Tales and Poems*
- Potok, Chaim *The Chosen*
- Sinclair, Upton *The Jungle*
- Steinbeck, John *The Grapes of Wrath*

- Stowe, Harriet Beecher *Uncle Tom's Cabin*
- Twain, Mark *The Adventures of Huckleberry Finn*
- Twain, Mark *The Adventures of Tom Sawyer*
- Twain, Mark *Innocents Abroad*
- Walker, Alice *The Color Purple*
- Washington, Booker T. *Up From Slavery*
- Wilder, Thornton *Our Town*

World Literature

- Austen, Jane *Pride and Prejudice*
- Austen, Jane *Sense and Sensibility*
- Bronte, Charlotte *Jane Eyre*
- Bronte, Emily *Wuthering Heights*
- Carroll, Lewis *Alice's Adventures in Wonderland*
- Cervantes, Miguel de *Don Quixote*
- Conrad, Joseph *Heart of Darkness*
- Defoe, Daniel *Robinson Crusoe*
- de Tocqueville, Alexis *Democracy in America*
- Dickens, Charles *Great Expectations*

- Dickens, Charles *David Copperfield*
- Dickens, Charles *Tale of Two Cities*
- Dostoevsky, Fyodor *Crime and Punishment*
- Dostoyevsky, Fyodor *The Gambler*
- Frank, Anne *The Diary of a Young Girl*
- Golding, William *Lord of the Flies*
- Hamilton, Edith *Mythology*
- Homer *The Iliad*
- Homer *The Odyssey*
- Hugo, Victor *Les Miserables*
- Huxley, Aldous *Brave New World*
- Kafka, Franz *Metamorphosis*
- L'Engle, Madeleine *A Wrinkle in Time*
- Lewis, C.S. *The Screwtape Letters*
- Machiavelli, Niccolo *The Prince*
- Marlowe, Christopher *Doctor Faustus*
- Milton, John *Paradise Lost*
- Orwell, George *Animal Farm*
- Plato *The Republic*
- Remarque, Erich Maria *All Quiet on the Western Front*

- Scott, Sir Walter *Ivanhoe*
- Shelley, Mary W. *Frankenstein*
- Shakespeare, William *Romeo and Juliet*
- Shakespeare, William *Twelfth Night*
- Sienkiewicz, Henryk *Quo Vadis: A Narrative of the Time of Nero*
- Solzhenitsyn, Alexander *One Day in the Life of Ivan Denisovich*
- Sophocles *Antigone*
- Stevenson, Robert Louis *The Strange Case of Dr. Jekyll and Mr. Hyde*
- Swift, Jonathan *Gulliver's Travels*
- Tolstoy, Leo *Anna Karenina*
- Tolkien, J.R.R. *The Hobbit*
- Tolstoy, Leo *War and Peace*
- Wells, H.G. *The Time Machine*
- Wells, H.G. *War of the Worlds*
- Wilde, Oscar *The Importance of Being Earnest*

Reluctant Readers

- Crane, Stephen *The Red Badge of Courage* (instead of *War and Peace*)

- Dostoyevsky, Fyodor *The Gambler*
- Hawthorne, Nathaniel *The Scarlet Letter* (instead of *Sense and Sensibility*)
- Hemingway, Ernest *Old Man and the Sea* (instead of *Moby Dick*)
- London, Jack *Call of the Wild*
- Melville, Herman *Billy Budd* (instead of *Moby Dick*)
- Shelley, Mary *Frankenstein*
- Steinbeck, John *Of Mice and Men*
- Steinbeck, John *The Pearl*

Kinesthetic learners

- London, Jack *Call of the Wild*
- Twain, Mark *The Adventures of Tom Sawyer*
- Twain, Mark *The Adventures of Huckleberry Finn*

Prolific Readers

- Austen, Jane *Jane Austen Four Novels* (Four of her best-loved novels: *Sense and Sensibility*, *Pride and Prejudice*, *Emma*, and *Northanger Abbey*)

- Tolkien, J. R. R. *J.R.R. Tolkien Boxed Set* (*The Hobbit* and *The Lord of the Rings*)
- Dickens, Charles *Major Works of Charles Dickens* (Penguin Classics set, includes *Great Expectations, Hard Times, Oliver Twist, A Christmas Carol, Bleak House, A Tale of Two Cities*

Popular Literature

- Stockett, Kathryn *The Help*

Word of Caution

All families are different, and therefore all families must decide their own standards for the books their children read. Some of these books are on almost every reading list, but that doesn't mean they are perfect for you. The books in this reading list are from a broad cross section of college-bound reading lists. However, parents assume all responsibility for their children's education. If you are not familiar with something on this list, please review the book first.

Conclusion

Choose Peace

Do you find yourself scrambling frantically to finish every problem in every book before you can relax for the summer? Instead, I encourage you to focus on choosing peace. Look at each subject you are trying to finish.

First ask, "Does it need to be done?" If you are 80% done with the book, that should be enough. Public schools complete 80% to finish the subject, and so can you.

Next ask, "Does it affect your mental health?" Weigh the pros and cons of finishing. At times, you will need to finish a book completely, but other times it's not required for high school credit, while the cost is enormous stress. Weigh the pros and cons!

If there is a subject you need to work on this summer, try to let your children work independently. Independently means you don't teach them, they learn on their own. If you need some accountability, have them show you their work from across the room, if necessary.

One mother told me her son avoided math most of the school year and was hopelessly behind — that's a good reason to continue math during the summer. Only do one lesson per day, not two! Choose peace!

Another friend I spoke to was stressed about starting French during the summer. It's not worth the stress! Unless you desperately need foreign language credits, choose peace! Skip that subject during the summer.

A dad asked about reading. Summer is a great time to snuggle up with a book, but don't worry about literary analysis.

Grab books from my College Bound Reading List in the previous chapter. Save those library receipts! That's how you'll collect all the information for the reading list in the coming year. Choose peace, and just enjoy reading this summer.

SAT preparation often happens in the summer. A little SAT prep each day keeps the skills fresh, and it doesn't require parental supervision — it's like a high school level workbook! Sure, work on some SAT prep during the summer. Keep it small, just one section per day, so kids don't rebel. Choose peace — one section per day is only half an hour, which is not too bad!

Summer is important. Remember to take a break. Think balance. Weigh what is important. Choose peace!

Appendix 1

End of School Year Popcorn Party Plan

When it's time to finish the school year, it can be difficult to feel "done." If you aren't completely done with a textbook or unit of study, you may want to think outside the box in order to finish classes quickly and still have time to enjoy summer.

If you want to finish quickly, consider finishing school with The Popcorn Party Plan.

Instead of sweating your way through the remainder of your textbook, groaning through every single assignment, go the quick and easy route instead. When you are ready to pull your hair out if you don't get a break soon, it's time to take evasive action. Find some educational videos to finish school. Remember, not every class in high school has to be difficult. I remember some high school classes that were significantly easier than others were! It's reasonable to decide right now that the class has been hard enough, so you can finish the easy way.

Finishing school with The Popcorn Party Plan will help you have fun AND finish school.

Scour the video section of your library, or talk to the librarian, to find supplemental videos that might address the final concepts in your textbook. Pop some corn, pop in the DVD, and you can finish the easy way. Make it a party setting, and celebrate the joy of homeschooling that gives you this flexibility. You can find videos that give a synopsis of history, algebra, biology, or health. You can use movies, documentaries, or lectures on DVD. Don't worry about doing everything the hard way. If you've been doing it the hard way all year, now is the time to homeschool the easy way, and just finish up so you can take a break.

Appendix 2

Finding a Summer Job

I was doing a Bible study on work and I remembered all the summers with my high school boys. It's so important to teach a strong work ethic! Take a moment with your teens and reflect on these verses. They could make great memory work and discussion topics before they take on a summer job.

God created man to work

"The LORD God took the man and put him in the Garden of Eden to work it and take care of it." Genesis 2:15

God works and we are created in His image.

"Jesus said to them, 'My Father is always at his work to this very day, and I too am working.'" John 5:17

Work is hard

"By the sweat of your brow you will eat your food until you return to the ground." Genesis 3:19

Work is satisfying

"The sleep of a laborer is sweet." Ecclesiastes 5:12

Work hard for the Lord

"Whatever you do, work at it with all your heart, as working for the Lord, not for human masters." Colossians 3:23

Work is key to a full life

"A sluggard's appetite is never filled, but the desires of the diligent are fully satisfied." Proverbs 13:4

We are also given warnings and examples

⁶ *"In the name of the Lord Jesus Christ, we command you, brothers and sisters, to keep away from every believer who is idle and disruptive and does not live according to the teaching you received from us. ⁷ For you yourselves know how you ought to follow our example. We were not idle when we were with you, ⁸ nor did we eat anyone's food without paying for it. On the contrary, we worked night and day, laboring and toiling so that we would not be a burden to any of you. ⁹ We did this, not because we do not have the right to such help, but in order to offer ourselves as a model for you to imitate. ¹⁰ For even when we were with you, we gave you this rule: "The one who is unwilling to work shall not eat." ¹¹ We hear that some among you are idle and disruptive. They are not busy; they are busybodies. ¹² Such people we command and urge in the Lord Jesus Christ to settle down and earn the food they eat. ¹³ And as for you, brothers and sisters,*

never tire of doing what is good. [14] Take special note of anyone who does not obey our instruction in this letter. Do not associate with them, in order that they may feel ashamed. [15] Yet do not regard them as an enemy, but warn them as you would a fellow believer." 2 Thessalonians 3.6-15

Set clear expectations for work during the summer months and help your child find a job this summer! Besides biblical instruction, there are so many other benefits! Your child can gain valuable experience by creating a resume and engaging in the interview process, not to mention valuable work experience! Both of my children began work in high school. My son Kevin taught chess. My son Alex worked in an office at a think tank in Seattle. You can include any summer job they do in high school on their transcript. All of this can be combined as an occupational education credit. It's the easiest class you will ever teach! Here is how to do it, in a simple no-muss, no-fuss way.

Simple Steps to Creating Your Occupation Education Credit

1. Wait until your child is motivated to make their own money

2. Your child will seek (or be forced to seek) a paying job

3. Count all your child's hours on the job

4. Once you count 150 hours, stop counting hours, and give one credit of Occupational Education for the year

5. Write a course description that includes job skills they learned

Transcript and Activity List

It's important to avoid double dipping with high school credit, recording each experience as just one high school credit. However, you can also list those experiences as activities. When I was in high school, I was involved in the choir. I received a high school music credit for the time I was in the class, but it was also an activity on my transcript.

On the transcript, highlight the most significant high school activities. If this summer activity were something important to the child, it would go first on the transcript. Indicate the year it was done, and if there was any special recognition or award for the activity. Just like my high school choir class was counted as a high school credit class and a high school activity, it's acceptable to have it listed both on the transcript as a class, and also list it within your activity list.

Ideas from Other Homeschoolers

I'm not the only one who managed to help their children find work in high school. I asked homeschoolers about the summer jobs their children experienced on my Facebook page. Here are some jobs other homeschoolers' children have worked on during the summer, from being an entrepreneur to working at a summer camp:

"Mine worked at a summer camp she's been going to for years as a camper. She loved it and plans to do it again next summer. The other one did a lot of babysitting. I helped connect her with one of the moms but she did the work well to keep the job." ~Debbie

"My daughter had babysitting- it was fun and hard work. My son had mowing, painting, and yard work." ~Michele

"My 15 year old girl spent the summer with her grandmother in another state working with her at an intercultural seminar they do every summer. She had a great time & learned so much. She met people from all over the world and she is ready to go back next summer." ~Julia

"My oldest worked at a Boy Scout camp and had a long, full schedule every week. He loved every minute of it and already plans to work there again next year." ~Evelyn

"My 12 year old son started a paper route in June and just finished his last day yesterday! Since we couldn't go anywhere all summer due to another child's activities this worked fine for us, but it turned out to be more work than he anticipated. Great lessons learned, though, in the value of working hard, being responsible, etc. He has wanted to earn money since he was quite young and last year asked about a paper route. I called the paper and had his name put on the list to call when a nearby route became available. My 14yo son mowed our neighbor's lawn once a week. Good job. This boy did not make nearly as much money as his 12 yr old brother." ~Angie

"My older daughter is working in a clothing store and will continue while she's in college." ~Sue

"My 16 year old daughter has been working for a gourmet popcorn shop. She runs their booth at our town's waterfront farmer's market each

Saturday for the summer and early fall. Tasty work!" ~Sheri

"My children are entrepreneurs. They raise and sell small livestock for meat." ~Sue

Afterword

Who is Lee Binz and What Can She Do for Me?

Number one best-selling homeschool author, Lee Binz is The HomeScholar. Her mission is "helping parents homeschool high school." Lee and her husband Matt homeschooled their two boys, Kevin and Alex, from elementary through high school.

Upon graduation, both boys received four-year, full tuition scholarships from their first choice university. This enables Lee to pursue her dream job - helping parents homeschool their children through high school.

On The HomeScholar website, you will find great products for creating homeschool transcripts and comprehensive records to help you amaze and impress colleges.

Find out why Andrew Pudewa, Director of the Institute for Excellence in Writing says, "Lee Binz knows how to navigate this often confusing and frustrating labyrinth better than anyone."

You can find Lee online at:

www.TheHomeScholar.com

If this book has been helpful, could you please take a minute to write us a quick review on Amazon?

Thank you!

Testimonials

Learn all you can!

"I joined the Gold Care Club, learned loads about junior year and homeschooling high school through the Club, and was able to prepare a transcript, go to a college fair, visit colleges, and finish my course descriptions.

Having Lee to advise you and hold your hand as you navigate the process will ensure success, as long as you do your part. She's helped me with two boys now, and both have been accepted to the colleges of their choice with scholarships.

I encourage you to learn all you can from Lee's materials and take advantage of all the support she has for you!"

~Ann in Connecticut

Weekly Discussion Calms Nerves

"Even though I am in the field of education, finding a plan for homeschooling high school and preparing good college transcripts was not easy. Then I came across Lee's website and everything changed. I joined the "Gold Care Club" and can't wait for my weekly discussion with Lee. I now feel confident that my daughter will have the necessary transcripts for graduating high school as well as the crucial transcripts for getting into the college of her choice."

~ Sue, mom to Brittany

For more information about my **Gold Care Club,** go to:

www.TheHomeScholar.com/Gold-Care.php

Also From The HomeScholar...

- The HomeScholar Guide to College Admission and Scholarships: Homeschool Secrets to Getting Ready, Getting In and Getting Paid (Book and Kindle Book)
- Setting the Records Straight - How to Craft Homeschool Transcripts and Course Descriptions for College Admission and Scholarships (Book and Kindle Book)
- Total Transcript Solution (Online Training, Tools and Templates)
- Comprehensive Record Solution (Online Training, Tools and Templates)

- Gold Care Club (Comprehensive Online Support and Training)
- Preparing to Homeschool High School (DVD)
- Finding a College (DVD)
- The Easy Truth About Homeschool Transcripts (Kindle Book)
- Parent Training A la Carte (Online Training)
- Homeschool "Convention at Home" Kit (Book, DVDs and Audios)

The HomeScholar Coffee Break Books Released or Coming Soon on Kindle and Paperback:

- Delight Directed Learning: Guiding Your Homeschooler Toward Passionate Learning
- Creating Transcripts for Your Unique Child: Help Your Homeschool Graduate Stand Out from the Crowd
- Beyond Academics: Preparation for College and for Life
- Planning High School Courses: Charting the Course Toward High School Graduation
- Graduate Your Homeschooler in Style: Make Your Homeschool Graduation Memorable

- Keys to High School Success: Get Your Homeschool High School Started Right!
- Getting the Most out of Your Homeschool This Summer: Learning just for the Fun of It!
- Finding a College: A Homeschooler's Guide to Finding a Perfect Fit
- College Scholarships for High School Credit: Learn and Earn With This Two-for-One Strategy!
- College Admission Policies Demystified: Understanding Homeschool Requirements for Getting In
- A Higher Calling: Homeschooling High School for Harried Husbands (by Matt Binz, Mr. HomeScholar)
- Gifted Education Strategies for Every Child: Homeschool Secrets for Success
- College Application Essays: A Primer for Parents
- Creating Homeschool Balance: Find Harmony Between Type A and Type Zzz...
- Homeschooling the Holidays: Sanity Saving Strategies and Gift Giving Ideas
- Your Goals this Year: A Year by Year Guide to Homeschooling High School

- Making the Grades: A Grouch-Free Guide to Homeschool Grading
- High School Testing: Knowledge That Saves Money
- Getting the BIG Scholarships: Learn Expert Secrets for Winning College Cash!
- Easy English for Simple Homeschooling: How to Teach, Assess and Document High School English
- Scheduling - The Secret to Homeschool Sanity: Plan You Way Back to Mental Health
- Junior Year is the Key to High School Success: How to Unlock the Gate to Graduation and Beyond
- Upper Echelon Education: How to Gain Admission to Elite Universities
- How to Homeschool College: Save Time, Reduce Stress and Eliminate Debt
- Homeschool Curriculum That's Effective and Fun: Avoid the Crummy Curriculum Hall of Shame!
- Comprehensive Homeschool Records: Put Your Best Foot Forward to Win College Admission and Scholarships
- Options After High School: Steps to Success for College or Career

- How to Homeschool 9th and 10th Grade: Simple Steps for Starting Strong!
- Senior Year Step-by-Step: Simple Instructions for Busy Homeschool Parents
- High School Math The Easy Way: Simple Strategies for Homeschool Parents In Over Their Heads

Would you like to be notified when we offer the next *Coffee Break Books* for FREE during our Kindle promotion days? If so, leave your name and email below and we will send you a reminder.

http://www.TheHomeScholar.com/
freekindlebook.php

Visit my Amazon Author Page!

amazon.com/author/leebinz

NOV 1 6 2017

Made in the USA
Columbia, SC
21 October 2017